Dirty Talk

A Step By Step Instructional Guide For Making Your Partner Pleasure Go Completely Nuts The Simplest Path To Mind-blowing Sexual Encounters For Both Men And Women

(To Help You Spice Up Your Love Life, Here Is A Beginner's Guide To Sexy Dirty Talking)

Jovan Fröschl

TABLE OF CONTENT

Taking On A Close Relative Or Friend's Trauma As Your Own When It Comes To Boundaries.....1

Communication As Well As The Planning Of It .4

The Model Of Complete Sexual Liberation.......20

Developing A Solid Bond Through Written Material..26

What Role Does Texting Play In Romantic Relationships?...33

Experiencing Love While Also Being Loved 40

Conversation About Sex: How To Approach The Subject Of Sexuality With Your Adolescent Child 43

My Child Shows Little Interest In Learning Anything New..55

How To Respond As A Parent To Your Child's Sexual Orientation Discussions............................62

How To Use Slutty Language To Sound More Seductive In Bed 85

Please Describe Your Objectives And The Driving Forces Behind Them 92

A Few Words About Giving Compliments 104

How To Be A Master In The Art Of Flirting With Her 115

Taking On A Close Relative Or Friend's Trauma As Your Own When It Comes To Boundaries

Hearing about the suffering or difficulty experienced by another person can be traumatic to your own neurological system. Even though you did not go through it yourself, you still feel pain, and this is especially true if you are closely related to the person who went through it. Simply put, this is how the nervous system operates. You and the other person will both experience discomfort as a result of your nerve systems becoming synchronized.

It is essential that you have this discussion with your daughter. She ought to be able to comprehend the fact that those with whom one shares intimate emotional connections suffer and are traumatized together. It's possible that she's heard that nurses in the medical care industry take on the trauma of the people for whom they are responsible.

The same thing happens with partners and close family members. If you've been through a traumatic experience, it's possible that it will make you appear to be a nasty person to others around you. At the very least, this is how your friends and family may perceive you when you begin behaving strangely or when you reach the point of exhaustion and completely collapse.

Your daughter may engage in irresponsible behavior and lack sympathy as a result of survival tactics. Tell her to stop, ask her to acknowledge what is taking place, and encourage her to step away for a while so she may work through the suffering.

In order for a young woman to be able to maintain herself as well as the people she loves while also taking the necessary precautions, it is highly crucial for her to establish boundaries throughout traumatic circumstances.

Communication As Well As The Planning Of It

The mechanics of having sex are rather straightforward, but having good sex is a very different kettle of fish. If you are reading this book, I will assume that you are interested in more than just basic performance in the bedroom. If that is the case, then you are in luck because the single most important rule of good sex is to never settle for bad, or even worse, boring sex.

The importance of communication, both verbal and nonverbal, cannot be overstated. If you've been following along, you should already be aware that paying attention to the cues, signals, wish list, smoke signals, and other communications sent by your partner is the most important element of the game.

And if you've been paying attention and taking pleasure in the sensations you've shared with your partner when flirting, making out, and engaging in foreplay, then you should have at least some notion of what they'd like at this stage of the process.

Are they in the kind of mood that says "take me now," or is the extended slow grove of an Al Green song more indicative of their disposition?

You alone will know, and you won't know anything until the time is right for you to do so.

You will be in a much better position to rise to the occasion if you maintain mental notes as you are traveling to this time and do yourself and your spouse a tremendous service by doing so.

The method: If you're interested in that sort of stuff, there are books published about sexual method, so feel free to look into it. For the sake of our discussion, I'm going to assume that you are more interested in actually carrying out the activity than in learning more about the activity through reading.

So I'm going to give you a map of sorts or more like a sexual GPS system that you can download into your brain and access according to the terrain you happen to be navigating, because here's the thing, human beings, while each is unique and precious, humans really aren't all that complicated, and there are a variety of physical and emotional signs which clearly indicate whether you're having good sex or not... So without further ado, let's get to it!

Putting the Body to Rest

It is important to make an effort to calm the body before engaging in tantric sex. It is very important to learn how to relax the body because, if you do not learn how to relax the body, you are going to feel a little weary and perhaps sick from the tension. After a difficult day, even if you didn't do a whole lot, it will feel as if you fought with a bear and lost. This is true even if you didn't do very much at all.

Relaxing the mind is just as vital as relaxing the body, so don't forget to do both while you're trying to unwind. Your immune system will become more compromised while you are under mental stress, which is exactly what germs and viruses want.

It is possible to become better at relaxing, but the most important thing to keep in mind is that you should not wander around as if you are lost in a cloud of Zen. However, you could be living in a scenario that causes chronic stress, and for many people, this has become the new normal. individuals frequently aren't aware of how stressed out they are, and the factors of debt, demands, and lack of coping abilities are frequently the cause of individuals becoming estranged from one another. Tantra helps you establish a bond that is closer than it has ever been, which for many people is about more than simply sex. This is a significant concept to comprehend because tantra helps you build a bond that is closer than it has ever been.

The idea of unwinding and relaxing might be challenging at times. You might have trouble finding a stress reliever that works over the long term, but taking a nap, taking a shower, or watching a movie that makes you laugh can undoubtedly help. You need to learn to accept that you're stressed out, and you need to spend time preparing yourself for this. Meditation is helpful, but it's an underrated practice. You also need to learn to accept that you're stressed out. If you're feeling a little down about the way that you appear, you should attempt to spend at least half an hour every day exercising or walking. You will find that it does, in its own unique manner, grant you freedom. Additionally, if you are relaxed, you will practice tantra much more effectively, and in the long run, you will be able to accept all of this.

The First Chapter

Are you looking for a form of entertainment that can actually bring you pleasure? It would be sufficient to watch a feel-good movie or read a suspense or romance novel. Have you tried to finish a book for many hours, but you just can't seem to get interested in it? Even after watching a marathon of the newest movies, do you feel that something is missing?

Have you ever given any attention to engaging in a sort of entertainment that is not all that typical? Do you have any idea what that is? For some, this may not be novel and may even appear to be the standard; yet, for others, this may be something fresh and, well, extremely exciting. I'm willing to bet that you already have an idea of what it is that I'm talking about. You are entirely correct in thinking that!

Adult DVDs can be a great way to kill boredom and provide a lot of laughs in the process. Check out how those hot women flashing their rear ends or those dudes prodding their shafts would pique your interest if you were feeling bored. Cheap porn DVDs can provide you with the exact level of fulfillment you're searching for, making them an excellent and exciting kind of entertainment that doesn't have to break the bank.

You would never believe your eyes if you saw a bunch of chicks doing the act together or a guy almost reaching his climax while the wild chick delivers him the best blow of his life. Those are the kinds of things that would blow your mind. If phrases like "ass to mouth," "the crab," and "the famous 'sixty-nine' position" aren't enough to rouse the wild animal that resides within you, you should make an appointment with a sex specialist as soon as you possibly can. Laugh it up! If you believe that you are not providing your partner with the hot and steamy sex session that he or she deserves, now is the time to make amends for it.

If you want to improve your Kama Sutra skills or if you want to learn sex positions that will undoubtedly transport you and your partner to the seventh heaven, XXX porn DVDs can be an excellent tutor for you to use. You can't wait to have the most amazing sex with your partner, can you?

Is it possible that you can't wait to hear her ask for more, more, and even more? Are you looking forward to the sound of your spouse groaning or screaming as you continue to go deeper and deeper inside of her? Then by all means, go ahead and purchase the naughtiest porn DVD download available on the internet, or just go ahead and get some porn DVDs that will take you to a very satisfying sexual life.

Studying the most effective sexual skills can turn you into a sex deity or put you on the path to being a sex expert. It's possible that one day you'll write your very own sex book that becomes an instant classic.

Because not everyone who watches titillating movies does so with the same purpose as stated above, there is no reason for you to feel shame when someone finds out that you keep porn DVDs because some people would just want to feed their curiosity and find out why a lot of people regardless of age, sex, and race are just so into these stuffs. This is why there is no reason for you to feel shame when someone finds out that you keep porn DVDs.

These kinds of videos are available to everyone who wants to see them, but it is important to keep in mind that possessing pornographic materials has with it some responsibilities, regardless of the reason you want to purchase them.

Have you ever considered the possibility that the role of testosterone in increasing desire and erection strength in males cannot possibly be the hormone's only involvement?

After a great deal of muttering, I finally manage to persuade Ford to come to my house so that we can discuss this matter. It's the only form of control I have over the situation. And I'm clinging to it by the skin of my teeth.

The fact that I want to let go is the thing that makes me feel the most unsettled.

Being able to look over Ford's shoulder was fun for me. It was funny when James paid attention to my rear end. When we finally got to the car, I really appreciated how carefully Heath assisted me down to the ground.

While I was riding in the backseat next to Heath, I overheard him respond to a text message from his father, in which the father explained that they would be unable to hang out with Heath because they had other commitments.

Me. I myself am the strategy. The possibilities make my chest tighten with excitement.

My original intention for the evening was to trade in my tight Santa outfit for a pair of sweatpants and a baggy t-shirt that I had stolen from Jameson a couple of years ago but he was unaware that I had done so. Even though I can no longer smell him, I enjoy being in close proximity to...him.

I also intended to put a scoop of mulling spices into the diffuser, simmer it in apple juice, and then put my feet up, cover them with fuzzy socks, and drink hot apple cider out of my favorite cup while watching the Hallmark Channel.

As I gently take the three of them up the stairs to my flat, my Plan A gives way to Plan B. If only I understood what steps were involved in Plan B.

As I stroll onto my personal balcony in the middle of the night, the ringtone that belongs to my mother reverberates through the air. Does she have some kind of parent radar that will alert her when we need to be reminded to treat one other with respect?

I dismiss the incoming call by clicking the screen.

Before I turn the key in the lock, I give the boys a look and tell them, "My house, my rules. Please refrain from picking on the younger sister. Please do not conspire against me. No—"

"We're not your obnoxious younger brothers like we used to be. We've come into our own. I swear to it. We are aware of how to behave around a lady. James gently rubs the palm of his hand across the side of my face, focusing on my cheek.

As I try to conjure up an interest, I feel a wave of wooziness sweep over me. Will I finally receive what I've been working toward for so many years? Could you please forgive them for all of the big brother jokes they made? Every part of me, down to my very cells, wants to put my faith in him.

As I face the entrance, I grab the doorknob, not only to unlock and open the door, but also for stability. I walk into the entry nook and gesture for the guys to proceed to the right, which is the direction that leads to the kitchen as well as the living room. The opposite path leads to a little hallway that has a bedroom and a bathroom off of it. I suppose the interior designer thought that if there was an official entryway, it would give the apartment a finer atmosphere.

While I secure the front door, Heath and Ford make themselves at home on my couch, while James waits for me in the foyer.

"You may proceed. Prepare to feel right at home.

The glimmer of curiosity that I had previously spotted is no longer a glimmer and has taken on a more naughtydemeanor. Is he restraining himself from making a taunt? I take a close look at him and notice that he has not altered the style of his bad boy hairstyle. It still has a side part and long bangs that drop down and brush against his eyes.

The Model Of Complete Sexual Liberation

Parents, take heart: contrary to what the media may try to convince you of, it is not inevitable that your teen will participate in risky sexual activity. Teens do have a choice, and with your guidance, your son or daughter can make an effort to make decisions that will serve them well in the years to come.

Despite the fact that abstaining from sexual activity goes against much of what our teenagers learn at their school and see in the media, it is still without a doubt the choice that is best for their health. The number of adolescents who engage in sexual activity is falling at a steady rate year after year, despite the fact that more deliberate and evidence-based educational initiatives are being put forward.[42]

Our children are paying attention, but it is important for them to be reminded of the same thing both at school and at home. They require that we maintain coherence between what we say and what we believe and what we tell them. We tell our teenagers that they can (and should) say no to smoking, drugs, and drinking for the benefit of their health; nevertheless, when it comes to sexual activity, we frequently take a different approach and presume that they are not capable of "just saying no."

Since the days when you had to take sex education — that is, if your school even offered any education at all — we have gone a long way. Through the decade of the 1980s, sexuality education in public schools across the United States was either nonexistent or labeled "nondirective." It was founded on the following four guiding principles:[43] Sexual activity during the adolescent years is unavoidable.

Regarding sexuality, educators should maintain an attitude of value neutrality.

Issues pertaining to sexuality should be discussed openly in schools.

Students should learn about birth control as part of their sexual education.

This "unbiased" approach had major repercussions, as it forced pupils into a mode of adult decision-making for which they were not yet emotionally or psychologically equipped. The teen population experienced both stress and perplexity as a result of it. And as a direct consequence of this, there has been a significant rise in the number of pregnancies and STDs experienced by adolescents as a direct result of sexual activity.

In the 1990s, out of concern for what was taking place and in response to the ongoing HIV pandemic, schools all over the country began to adopt a more prescriptive method of teaching about sexuality in the classroom. The directive teaching method does not try to scare teenagers into making healthy choices; rather, it educates them with evidence that is correct from a medical standpoint regarding the long-term repercussions of underage sexual engagement. When the directive approach is used in the right way, teens are able to understand a variety of concepts, including but not limited to the following: how to set boundaries, how to say "no," how to set goals, the differences between the characteristics of a healthy relationship and the characteristics of an unhealthy relationship, the benefits of making the decision to abstain from sexual activity, the reality of the risks and consequences that are associated with teen sexual activity, and more.

The model that I use to instruct directive sexual education is called the Pure Sexual Freedom model, and it's based on the premise that every person who chooses to date, including your teen son or daughter, deserves to have a dating experience that is both healthy and pleasant. I teach this model to parents who want to teach their children how to have healthy, positive dating experiences. The concept of a healthy relationship, as well as its outward appearance and the components that make up its makeup, are defined by Pure Sexual Freedom. We show young people that a good dating relationship is only possible if the two people involved have compatible values, respect themselves and each other, and choose to act in a way that is actually beneficial to the other person in all aspects of their life, including their physical health, their mental well-being, their financial situation, and their social relationships.

Developing A Solid Bond Through Written Material

Spending quality time with another person is widely regarded as one of the most important factors in the development of a relationship between two people. On the other hand, by taking measures to reduce the number of social activities and get-togethers, many of us may be preventing ourselves from engaging in any future love endeavors out of the concern that a "long-distance relationship" may result in nothing but disappointment.

Do not confine yourself solely to the confines of this framework, despite the undeniable fact that having a physical connection is essential to the development of a relationship. Long before this time, many people have been successful in maintaining relationships despite the distance between them, which is proof that it is possible! Since you are unable to continue spending time together in person, you will most likely communicate with one another through text messages for the foreseeable future. The following are some tactics that can be used to cultivate a budding friendship through the use of text messages.

Don't break the rhythm!

Texting is a form of conversation in the same sense that talking to someone face to face is. When it comes to preserving a certain degree of communication, the flow of the conversation is really essential. A break in the flow of the conversation, just as in a face-to-face encounter, can cause unease and give the impression of apathy.

It could be difficult to proceed with the conversation if the ball is passed to one person and that person does not pass it on when it is their turn to receive it. Make an effort to leave the other person with a question or statement to which they can respond. This will give the impression that you want the discussion to continue for longer, and it will encourage the opposing side to respond.

Emoticons and stickers should be used.

It can be challenging to communicate effectively via text because neither party is able to see the other's facial expressions nor hear the other's tone of voice. Texting alone might lead to misunderstandings in communication. Emojis are used to communicate feelings and provide context for the tone of the sender. Make the most of the wide variety of visually appealing stickers and GIFs that are currently available and use them to your advantage to add emphasis to the tone of the message you are sending. Additionally, it is a great way to make your texting companion smile, which is another benefit of using this feature.

Dig down low

Are you running out of material to talk about? Texting can quickly get boring if you engage in useless, inconsequential chats with your friends that don't seem to go anywhere.

There is just so much that one person can share about their day. Make the most of this opportunity to dissolve some barriers and have a conversation on more profound topics. Initiate a conversation with them about their thoughts on larger issues, or take part in a discussion about current events.

You may be able to increase the amount of information you have about him or her and better comprehend them as a result of this. Because it gives them more time to consider their responses, some people find that communicating by text is more comfortable for them when discussing sensitive topics than doing so in person. Additionally, it might lessen the discomfort factor and make it easier for the two of you to open out to each other.

Make use of a complement

Everybody likes praise. Compliments are a great way to show that you are paying attention to and appreciating the qualities of your partner. By making personal and real comments to your texting friend, you might increase the likelihood that they will associate the feeling of closeness and camaraderie with you.

A compliment is another tool that can help you get out of the "buddy zone" metaphorically speaking. Complimenting someone by text is obviously more difficult than doing it in person because you might not be able to comment on their physical characteristics.

Consider aspects of their persona or character that you admire in them, and then mention those aspects in your discussion about them. Complementing someone on their personality is just as flattering as complimenting them on their appearance, if not more so.

What Role Does Texting Play In Romantic Relationships?

It is a way to maintain some sort of connection with your partner even when the two of you are not physically there with one another.

Some industry experts are of the opinion that the reasons for engaging in sexting while in a relationship may vary according to the type of connection that exists. There are three distinctly different types of connections:

•When people are securely connected to one another, it is simple and pleasant to get closer to one another. • Individuals who are restlessly joined frequently worry about being let go and may have the need to completely merge their lives with those of another person. Restlessly joined people don't stress out as much over giving up.

- Those who are avoidantly connected find it difficult to become close to other people and have trouble sharing personal information with their closest allies.

According to research, those who have connection styles that are avoidant or restless may be more likely to engage in the practice of sexting. Sexting is a form of electronic messaging that allows users to send and receive text messages electronically rather than sending and receiving voice calls. Sexting is a form of electronic messaging that allows users to engage in sexual activity while maintaining a physical distance from their partner.

Studies have shown that young adults who are not involved in long-term relationships nonetheless engage in the practice of sexting with their partners and potential partners.

The following is a list of emoticons that you may find useful to include in your text messages:

•The water drop emoticon is useful when you want to let your partner know that you're getting wet or that you're about to roll to come. You can use this emoticon in the same context as the rolling to come emoticon. You can also use it in a more limited capacity if you so choose. For example, if your partner were to give you a photo that was particularly appealing, you could use this emoticon as part of your response to convey that the photo was stimulating your sexual desire.

•The heart-eye emoticon is an easy way to indicate your partner that you are enjoying what they are saying or doing while you are simultaneously sexting. It is also a great way to signal that you are paying attention to what they are saying or doing.

•The slobbering emoticon conveys to your partner that you are actually slobbering and are also extremely turned on by everything that they are doing. This emoticon is similar to the heart-eye emoji in that it implies that you are extremely turned on by what they are doing.

•The tongue sticking out to the side of your face emoticon: The essential message conveyed by this emoticon is "Yum." One more wonderful argument for endorsing your partner's point of view.

•The mind blown emoticon should be used when your co-conspirator's texting skills are so impressive that they blow your mind. Or, on the other hand, for when you're recounting how your partner completely blew your mind the other night.

•If this emoticon could talk, it would tell you to "Hold up!" if it were the eyes emoji. If this emoticon could talk. Because you are paying such close attention to what you are viewing or reading, you should think of it as your eyes playing tricks on your mind.

•Smiley face with flames: A fantastic way to let your partner know that you think they are smoking hot in front of others.

•Villain emoticon: This is a good emoticon to sprinkle towards the end of your sexts in order to cause them to feel more energetic and underhanded.

•The Heavenly Messenger Emoticon: This is another emoticon that is great for adding to the furthest boundary of a sext, particularly if you are probing or playing shy/accommodating from the beginning of the conversation.

•Monkey emoticon: Are you looking back on your most recent solicitation or sext with a sense of shame or modesty? You can demonstrate this by using this emoticon, which is available.

•Eggplant emoticon: Despite the fact that this emoticon is far too boring to ever think of using in your sexts, it would be inappropriate not to include it on this list given that it is commonly referred to as the phallus emoticon (the banana and Champagne emoticons receive excellent notices). A vibrator in the form of an eggplant emoji is actually available for purchase.

•Peach emoticon: Another emoticon that is a little bit ridiculous, but the peach is undoubtedly the best emoticon to use if you want to express your sweetheart's derriere using an emoticon structure.

•Swimming man emoji: If you are in a playful mood, you can include this emoticon when you are describing to your vaginal-having companion how you are going to orally please them (you are going to get her so wet that you are going to be swimming in her pussy; get it?). Assuming you are in a playful mood, you can use this emoticon.

Experiencing Love While Also Being Loved

The very greatest form of RELATIONSHIP is one in where both parties are able to have fun with one another and not take things too seriously all the time. When it's only the two of you, it's okay to act childish with each other since you won't be judged for it.

You can threaten to fight each other and then ask the other person if they want to engage in physical conflict with you. You can make fun of each other by joking around and competing to determine whose quip is the most disrespectful.

You may make fun of each other and poke fun at each other's anxieties and then explain that you were joking afterward because you adore what it is that makes the other person insecure.

You two can keep each other laughing all day long with inside jokes and references that you both made up.

What's the point of being in a relationship if you can't laugh together?

Regrettably, in the race of life – to earn more, to accomplish more, and to get more – we often find ourselves. WE CANNOT WIN. We miss out on the most important experience in life, which is to love and to be loved.

Love is something to be experienced and realized; it is not something to be controlled.It is not about dominance but rather learning. If it can be controlled, it cannot be loved; rather, it is a concession that the other person is making on your behalf in order to meet your needs. Get out from under that delusion. Get rid of the things and people you don't like being around.

Conversation About Sex: How To Approach The Subject Of Sexuality With Your Adolescent Child

You should never anticipate that your kid will be the one to start a talk like that.

It is always necessary for you to get things started. A child's inquiry into these matters may lead adults to speculate or believe that the youngster is already engaging in the activity, despite the fact that this is highly unlikely to be the case.

You can begin this discussion in a number of different ways, one of which is by just doing it in an informal environment.

I once witnessed a father and a daughter go on a lunch date outside of their home to have a conversation about guys, and yes, she was very enthusiastic about the topic she had with her father. I also saw that the father was pleased with the conversation he had with his daughter.

Therefore, whatever you believe would put them more at ease helps making it easier to have such a conversation. This makes it easier to engage in.

It's also possible that you may start the topic with your child by inviting them to help you make supper or wash the dishes. From there, you could have such a chat with your kid.

When you chat to them, avoid using any tone that could be construed as judgmental because doing so will only result in you blowing your cover and possibly having to live with the regret of having done so.

Employing a tone that is more conversational helps to calm your audience, which in turn makes it easier for them to respond to any questions you may ask. This, in turn, serves to set the stage for the dialogue about the topics on which you need to educate your audience.

When you also observe that your child is hanging out with a particular person of the opposite sex, you may simply and casually ask inquiries about what your child has been up to and also inquire about the whereabouts of such a person.

This helps to establish the groundwork for another talk that you and your child can have.

And if, after trying all of these different things, none of them work, what then?

Simply telling an old story would do the task just fine.

Discuss who you are and what you've been through, then share your experiences with others. You can simply have a good chuckle by talking about some of the negative things first to let them know that you were also in their shoes. This will let them know that you can empathize with them.

As soon as you are able to do this, you will have a more intimate relationship with your adolescent child, which will make it much simpler for you to assist them in obtaining an education regarding their sexuality and sex.

Always keep in mind that this is not about you, but about them, and that knowing and comprehending this will assist ensure that you put them first while talking to them and that you never have to be judgmental about what they tell you.

Being judgemental puts an end to it all since you won't be able to have such an audience with them again, and the purpose of these interactions is to ensure that these conversations are continuing so that they may ask you questions and receive advice from you while knowing that you won't go nuts on them for doing such things. Being judgmental puts an end to it all.

Find Out If She Is Interested in You and How to Tell

There are several telltale signals that might assist you in determining whether the woman you are messaging is interested in you. If you are unsure of this, you should look for these signs. In the next section, we will instruct you on how to determine whether or not she has an interest in you. There are also a few things you can say to her in a text message that will pique her interest in you, which is useful if you want to take the conversation to the next level.

If she responds to you within a few minutes, you can assume that she is interested in what you have to say. It's possible that she was extremely busy and only now saw your message; on the other hand, it's also possible that she truly wants to chat to you.

If you have the impression that she is flirting with you as well, it is a strong indicator that she has an interest in you. This in no way indicates that she is prepared for a date or a sexual connection of any kind. To the point when she thinks she's ready to take things to the next level, a little flirting now and again might sometimes move her closer to that place. If you and your companion have moved on from one subject to another in the course of your discussion, you might be heading in the direction of something more significant. If you start chatting to her about more personal subjects, you run the risk of having this happen.

If she is trying to get more personal with you by asking questions about your life or making predictions about what you would do in a given situation, then this is usually an indication that she's interested in you. For example, if she asks you what you would do in a certain situation or asks you about your life, then she may be interested in you. We humans are naturally quite inquisitive. If we did not find the other person interesting, we would not go to the trouble of asking them so many questions.

If she brings up her future plans while she's chatting to you, there's a strong likelihood that she wants to include you in those plans. Perhaps she is planning a trip or is considering a career change at this time. These things frequently result in the beginning of new adventures and connections with other individuals. If it seems as though all she wants to know about is the specifics of your life and she is at ease sharing her own with you, then it is possible that you will be embarking on an exciting journey with her.

It's possible that she's starting to plan out when she'll next get to see you. This is one of the most significant indicators that she might be interested in you as a potential partner. If you spend time together, she will want to get together with you again in the future. This can be a clue that she likes you or wants to get to know you better.

It's possible that she's relaying all of this information to you because she's aware that if you're interested in her, then there's a strong probability that she should investigate whether or not things are serious between the two of you. If she is trying to get personal with you, then there is a good chance that the two of you have more in store for each other in the future.

When people start getting into the mindset of being in a relationship, the next step for the majority of them is to talk about their goals for the future. This sort of thing being said by women is not unheard of by any means, but it does happen far less frequently than it does by men. The majority of women are interested in hearing how your relationship is doing. If you give off the impression that you are enthusiastic and interested in her, there is a strong probability that she is beginning to feel the same way about you.

If she is considering how the two of you could spend the rest of your lives together, then this is excellent news for the two of you. It's possible that she likes you and wants to start a relationship with you soon, so take this as a hint that she's interested in you. If there are a lot of these kinds of thoughts exchanged over text, then it's more probable that there is something significant about the two of you moving forward together. This might happen when women start thinking about their hopes and aspirations for their shared future.

If she is starting to discuss some of her ambitions with you, then it is a sign that she is getting closer to the beginning of a relationship with you. It's possible that she has ambitions that she's never discussed with anyone else. It's possible that she's never shared any of this information with anyone else before, and this is one of the first times she's done so. When women are ready for a committed relationship, they will begin communicating things like this with their partners, such as how they feel about the relationship.

It's possible that she feels the same way about you if you know that something is about to happen and you can't wait for it to happen. This could be an indication that she likes you. It's possible that she has something, like a date or a sexual encounter, planned for the two of you to do together in the near future. Sometimes all that women desire from their guys is to have a sexual encounter with them.

My Child Shows Little Interest In Learning Anything New.

Even though some children may not ask a lot of questions about sexuality and relationships, this does not necessarily mean that they are not interested in the subject.

It's possible that they got the memo that asking about this isn't a smart move on their part.

If anything like this happens, it is incumbent upon you to take the initiative and bring the issue up on your own. You are making it very plain to your youngster that this is a subject about which you take pleasure and are well prepared to engage in conversation.

The topic should not be discussed with young children.

Children are exposed to sex-related subjects at a far earlier age than they should be given today's sexualized atmosphere in which children are raised.

When your child begins interacting with other children, attending to school, using the internet, listening to mainstream music, and watching television, movies, or cartoons, they will be exposed to sex messages. This exposure is unavoidable.

This suggests that they may approach you with questions regarding what they have heard in the future. Children are typically curious about sexuality at a variety of ages and stages throughout their development. They begin by being curious in the origin of children, then move on to the process by which infants are developed, and then turn their attention to sexual activity as their level of comprehension increases.

The problem is that it's possible that they've heard about certain things (like oral sex) before getting interested in the different ways that we could communicate sexual attraction to one another. Children are exposed to sexually explicit material on a daily basis, even though they are not developmentally ready for it. It's only natural for children to be curious about things that are above their comprehension level.

It is your duty as a parent to provide your child an answer that is suitable for his or her age in response to a question that is obviously inappropriate for that age.

It is very important that you respond to your child's question because they need to know that they can rely on you as a reliable source of knowledge.

If they come to you with questions, you have the opportunity to give them with information that is suitable for their age and will assist them in processing the sexualized signals to which they are exposed on a daily basis!

A Step-by-Step Guide to Transform Your Bravery Into Confidence

Choose one facet of your life that you feel could use some work and focus on that. This could include practicing your interview skills, turning more sales, striking up conversations with attractive women, or even taking the stage. Ask yourself: If you were to find yourself in any of these predicaments, would it be necessary for you to develop more courage or confidence? Now, picture how your ideal self would go about gaining the bravery and self-assurance necessary to excel in the area of your life that you have selected. What would happen if you only took a tenth of the actions that your ideal self had performed to get to where she is now? What specific steps do you need to take? Check out my blog at for other suggestions on how to boost your self-assurance.

Try to work up the gumption to say "thank you" to the cashier the next time you are waiting in line at the grocery store. They will appreciate it. If you really want to take it to the next level, you should inquire about how she spent her day. The most important thing you can do is integrate all facets of social competence into your daily life. Maintaining your self-assurance requires you to consistently behave in a self-assured manner.

Describe at least five current sources of self-assurance that you have at your disposal. In the event that you do not have five, describe the ones that you do have. How does this compare to other investments in terms of return on investment? To put it another way, how has this source enabled you to increase your improvement quotient without actually making an effort to do so? For instance, going to the gym not only helps you become more disciplined, but it also makes you more attractive to people of the opposite sex and increases your capacity to handle discomfort. These three advantages come from relying on a single source of confidence. If you find that the sources you are using to solve this issue aren't as effective as the example of the gym, you may either add a few more sources or consider replacing the ones you are using with ones that are more effective. This activity is totally open to personal interpretation. If you believe that watching anime helps you improve your Japanese language abilities and provides you with topics to talk about with your friends, then it might become a legitimate source of confidence for you.

How To Respond As A Parent To Your Child's Sexual Orientation Discussions

The experience of parenting a child who has a different sexual orientation than one's own might come with its own set of distinct obstacles. The following is some advice for parents who are dealing with the sexual orientation of their child:

-Have a conversation with your kid about their experiences and how they're feeling. It is essential to cultivate an atmosphere that is both open and secure for your kid, so that they can talk about their sexuality without feeling self-conscious.

Become informed about the many sexual orientations that are. This will assist you in better understanding your child as well as the emotions that they are experiencing.

- Always show your youngster that you are willing to embrace and support them. They need your love and support more than anything else, especially right now.

-Inspire your child to stay loyal to who they are while also being kind to others. They should not have to compromise who they are or their right to live an authentic life because they deserve it.

- Speak with other parents who have children with a variety of sexual orientations and identities. They are capable of providing insightful advice and support.

The role of a parent is never an easy one, but it is essential to keep in mind that your child requires your love and support regardless of the circumstances.

If you are having trouble accepting the sexual orientation of your child, you should seek the assistance of a professional. Your child is deserving of love and acceptance precisely because of who they are.

It is natural for a parent to feel protective of their child and the future they have planned for them.

You hope that they can avoid being harassed and discriminated against so that they can live a happy and successful life.

It is crucial to keep in mind that even while it may be challenging to acknowledge the fact that your child does not identify as heterosexual, this does not alter who they are as a person.

They are still the beautiful person that you have always loved and cared for, and nothing has changed about that.

There are a few significant things that you can do to help support your child, including the following:

- Hear what they have to say: Give them the opportunity to talk to you about their experiences and how they are feeling without you passing judgment. They will have a greater sense of being loved and supported as a result of this.

- Always be present for them: Let them know that you will always be there for them, whatever the situation may be. Having this will give you a sense of security even when things are difficult.

Even though sexual orientation might be a touchy subject, it is essential that you foster an environment in which your child feels free to express themselves openly and without fear of reprisal. You will be able to assist them in experiencing joy and love for who they are as a result of your actions.

Men's thoughts about women are typically negative.

Women are magnificent beings, not only in the eyes of men, but also in the eyes of the rest of the world. This is a truth that cannot be denied. Have you ever failed to notice that even the elderly man's eyes turn in her direction whenever a stunning woman goes by? When a man focuses his attention on a woman, particularly in an emotionally or sexually charged setting, he simply is unable to remove her from his thoughts, even if the task at hand requires him to maintain the utmost concentration.

Now that we know that women have this ravenous influence on males in general, the question is: when a man finally manages to have that lady all to himself, does he go on to thinking about other important things? You are aware that if you successfully hook a man on something, there is no way for him to quit, and the plan will be a success if you are successful in doing so. You can be sure that he is still thinking about you every waking moment, but what can you do if you are unable to pin him down? Because he is a physical entity, it is only natural to assume that he will be thinking about other people at some point or another.

Which is More Important—Appearance or Personality?

At first, it will almost certainly be more about your looks than it will be about your personality for a guy, but that does not necessarily mean that your looks won't matter. I am aware that this sounds revolting, but the primary reason behind this is that males are inherently vain until an intelligent lady such as yourself comes along and enlightens his brain. When he is able to think creatively, it indicates that he is aware that there must be something more than just appearance for two people to get along well, and this is when personality comes into play.

If you ask a guy who has been forced to split up with a really hot girlfriend what occurred, he will tell you that there was always a personality conflict between the two of them. Personality, on the other hand, is what will keep you there even after your good looks have gotten you through the door to him. The bright side is that even though you can't alter your physical appearance, you can always work on developing your personality.

Influence of Others? No...A Friendship That Is Valued.

When dating a guy, there are occasions when you become aware of the significant impact that his friends have on him. Often, this occurs without your knowledge. Even if you would be tempted to judge irrationally and label it as peer pressure, for him, that constitutes a friendship that is appreciated. The opinion of his friend is more important than you may realize. A great deal more. When you are trying to make a good first impression on a guy, you should keep in mind that it is not enough to simply win over the guy himself; you also need to win over his buddies.

The conclusion can be reached without providing any further explanation. You are now aware that his friends have the ability to either strengthen or weaken your connection. Even if you put in a lot of effort to make a good impression, there are certain friends who will always be willing to do all in their power to ruin your chances of getting together with the person you want. It's possible that they just don't like you, but more than likely it's because you got off to a bad start with them. Both explanations are possible.

Think at it this way: if the rest of the crew does not find you beautiful, it is possible that his perception of your attractiveness will change overnight as well. If a guy's buddies keep telling him that dating the female in question isn't such a good idea, then it's possible that he'll suddenly lose interest in the girl, despite the fact that he may actually have feelings for her.

You ought to be aware of the fact that rather than making an effort to lessen the impact of peer pressure, it is in your best interest to find a way to turn it to your advantage. If he tells you, "this is my man," pay attention to what he's saying and take it to indicate that whenever he's not around, you should consider this to be my immediate cover story.

Is It Typical to Lose Sexual Attraction to One's Partner?

When a love relationship first starts, there is frequently a powerful magnetic connection between the two people involved. Every kiss is exciting and full of passion, every private moment is intense, and it appears as though the first physical yearning will always be there.

However, in all honesty, such early charm can never be maintained over the course of time. It is completely appropriate for the expression of your feelings for your spouse to take place in methods that are not characterized by excessive sensuality. If, on the other hand, you completely lose interest in your relationship, this is unquestionably not a development that you want to see happen. It's possible that when the initial spark of attraction wore out, you started taking it for granted and assuming it would last for the rest of your life. But putting forth effort is necessary for even the most intimate of relationships.

Because of this, you and your spouse should discuss the lack of attraction that has developed between you. In certain circumstances, having dialogues that are mindful may help improve the situation, however in other circumstances, emotional counseling is required. The approaches that can be taken to resolve the issue are diverse and dependent on the factors that led to the decreased attraction.

People are strange creatures.

She was so repulsed by her behavior that it caused her to frequently become violently ill afterward. Her behavior was so at odds with the rest of her personality as well as the moral and cultural ideas that she held. According to conventional opinion, the issue should not have persisted after she had discovered the source of the problem during hypnosis sessions and been given the green light to end her promiscuity after being assured she could do so.

It did in a roundabout way. She continued to believe that she was worthless, but she was informed and given a potent post-hypnotic suggestion that she is unable to participate in sexual activity outside of the context of a committed relationship.

But despite this, she remained gorgeous and continued to attract the attention of the males whom she had previously inspired to belittle her.

Amy's solution to this conundrum was to start putting on weight. Eating herself into obesity to prevent herself from breaking the no sexual activity rule in a vain attempt to fulfill the criteria. Because no one had addressed her underlying and entirely baseless sentiments of unworthiness, her mind handled an otherwise irresolvable situation in this way. She did not do this consciously, but it was how her mind dealt with the issue.

After three years of treatment that was unsuccessful, her psychologist reached out to a mutual acquaintance, who then reached out to me.

Because Amy's psychologist is someone who has earned my respect, it came as a surprise to me that no one had considered addressing the primary issue. They had merely covered it up and diverted her attention away from it, but they had never genuinely done anything to boost her sense of self-worth.

Following a chance encounter with her, I made up my mind to address the issue by having sexual relations with her personally.

In point of fact, it is not the case. Although I never intended for us to get romantically involved, that is exactly what happened. Due to the fact that I am not trained in mental health, I am free to propose thoughts and hypotheses that, if spoken by someone who is trained in the field, would get that person fired. I was also in a position to provide a solution to the issue that no one else could: I altered the memories that had led her to believe that she was worthless.

In the end, this resulted in the creation of the Relyfe Programming model. Early on, I realized that it would be impossible to reframe all of the memories there were. The erroneous notion that she is flawed by sin and will always be imperfect led the poor child to believe that others are, or at the very least might be, more deserving than she is. As a result, the child spent the majority of her life believing that she was unworthy. She also held one of the most harmful ideas there is, which is that in this life, God rewards those who are worthy and punishes those who are not worthy.

I make it a point to steer clear of discussing religion in public, but I have to state that simply isn't how things operate. I am not in a position to confirm or deny the possibility that God occasionally intervenes in the lives of individuals; nevertheless, I can say with certainty that while we are still in this world, He does not consistently reward or punish people based on their degree of deservingness. Believe me, I am aware of it.

Kind There were just too many memories, spanning thirty years' worth of time, trying to convince Amy that God wasn't doing His job in putting her into the gutter, so she needed to do it before He noticed. Amy's subconscious saw that she was being rewarded when she felt singularly unworthy, and was still seeing these worthy folk at her hospital suffering.

Making plans to have sex

Although it eliminates the element of surprise, planning sexual encounters can be beneficial for couples who want to keep their sexual lives on track. Whether it is a date night planned a week in advance or simply stating "Hey, let's have sex tomorrow night," the anticipation that builds as you look forward to that special time together is just as much of a part of the fun as the pleasure that you will experience during the act itself. Send a message to your spouse letting them know that you are unable to hold off until later on in the day.

Privacy

There are some couples that I know that designate their bedroom as a "kid-free zone," meaning that their children are not permitted to enter the room under any circumstances unless it is an emergency. You also have the option of putting a lock on the door, asking the children to knock before entering, or explaining to them that their parents will occasionally need some quiet time to themselves. It took me a long time to figure out that my parents made my sibling and I a big lunch on Sunday afternoons consisting of fufu and chicken soup, and then they sent us away to nap so that they could spend some quality time together without us interrupting them.

Getting one's feet wet

Make the most of the brief intervals of time that you have available to spend together. Conduct a speedy session during a time when the youngsters are occupied doing something else. Take use of the opportunity to touch one another. Make out as you did when you were first married. Kiss passionately.

Make the Most of Your Networks

Set up play dates with friends or organize a babysitting network with your local pals so that you may take turns looking after each other's children. This will provide parents the much-needed opportunity to spend some time alone together.

Talk to each other.

If you are a woman and you have pain during sexual activity, it is important for you to communicate your discomfort honestly. Things may have altered for you during pregnancy or after childbirth, and it may take some time for you to fully recover. Take things slowly and make sure there is enough of lubrication involved until you feel like you can handle more.

Care for oneself

When you feel good about how you look, you look nice. Put in some effort to seem presentable, more for the benefit of yourself than of anyone else. Investing some time in getting dressed and doing your hair in the morning can have a significant impact on how you think and feel throughout the rest of the day.

Coins and tokens.

It's the details that matter, not the big picture. When my spouse gives me a cup of tea, it always puts a huge smile on my face. Even if he does not drink tea himself, he takes the effort to do something simple that will make me smile even though he knows it will make me happy. This demonstrates to me that he is thinking of me. A sign of appreciation, regardless of how meager it may be, is a wonderful method to convey to your partner that you value and cherish them, no matter how little it may be.

The law that governs motion

The first law of motion developed by Isaac Newton states that an item in motion will continue moving unless it is pushed upon by a force that is imbalanced. Therefore, if you engage in frequent sexual activity, you will continue to engage in sexual activity on a regular basis. Make it a regular part of your life together as a married couple. Get back on the horse as soon as possible if you fall off of it, before it gets too difficult to even try to complete the mission.

Sexual Activity and Pregnancy

It is quite safe to continue having sexual relations during your pregnancy, unless your doctor specifically advises you not to do so. Because the infant is protected by the uterus, sexual activity cannot harm the unborn child. As a result of the rise in hormone levels that occurs during pregnancy, some women experience an increase in their libido during this time. Because pregnant women may more easily support their bumps in some positions, such as the woman-on-top position, spooning, and the doggie style, certain positions may be more comfortable for pregnant women. Later on in the pregnancy, sexual activity might bring on contractions known as Braxton Hicks, which are harmless to the unborn child.

How To Use Slutty Language To Sound More Seductive In Bed

The best way to figure out what a sexual partner needs or wants is to be open with one another and talk about it. Talk about your sexual fantasies with your partner, tell them what you want to hear from them, and you'll find that both your intimate encounters and your romantic partnerships improve.

Dirty chat could make you feel awkward at first, but if done correctly, it has the potential to completely transform your sexual life. The following are a few suggestions that will assist you in sounding sexier in conversation and translating that quality into your sexual life.

a) You need to be in the proper frame of mind to engage in nasty discussion. One common error that lovers make is that they make too much of an effort to sound "hardcore" or "gangster" without actually believing what they mean by those words. The most crucial aspects are practicing deep breathing and conducting tests, but you also need to make sure you're heading in the proper direction. Be quick, be relaxed, and above all else, be communicative.

b) Begin by making the sound "purr" or "hmmm," maintain a normal breathing pattern, and then accompany the sounds with appropriate physical touches such as stroking and soft liking. Your spouse will answer before things get too serious between the two of you. Remind your partner that feedback is an essential part of the topic creation process, and then urge them to move on.

c) Stay informed about your friend's current situation. Restate well-known sayings in a seductive manner. This love boost is enhanced by whispering and emphasizing certain phrases, such as "let me know what to do... your word is my order." d) Avoid arguing with what your spouse says or does because it can be a mood killer if you have the ability to do so. Everyone has their own obscene manner of talking, and even if you disagree with it, you may maintain your politeness. If you don't like the name that they call you, you may, for instance, respond with "oh, yeah, that's right......or better yet call me xxxx" and then proceed to use the alternative name.

e) It is not hard to recognize when someone is excited, but there is no point in seeking advice if you do not intend to act on it. Ask your partner what they want from you, and keep in mind the things they say that boost your confidence. However, you shouldn't push the envelope, and you should be aware of the boundaries that you don't have to break. Some people only go so far as to ruin an exciting and sexual moment.

You're both going through similar experiences, but she's not receptive to the other guy's advances.

You can't be effective at dirty conversation if you don't understand the difference between the two.

But before we go any farther and start thinking about the many kinds... To begin, you and I need to consider the reasons why males tend to engage in inappropriate behavior when in bed. After all, a lot of guys don't do that, so there's no reason for you to start now.

If you want your wife to be sexually satisfied with you, it is imperative that you engage in lewd conversation with her in the bedroom of your home every time you engage in sexual activity with her.

You are obviously aware of the fact that having sex is an extremely MENTAL EXPERIENCE for women. In contrast, most men experience sexual activity primarily as a purely physical process.

The idea behind this is simple, but it's really important: you should give your girlfriend, who is so powerful, the BEST SEX EVER and the orgasms she shouts for... Not only does it have to be stimulated, but so does the woman's mind as well as her uterus.

And while you're in the shower, you're keeping your wife's mind active by talking about inappropriate things.

Because they are AFRAID, many guys try to steer clear of conversations like this one. In other words, they were cowards when it came to the bedroom.

Many men steer clear of using vulgar language since they have experimented with it in the past and found that it did not achieve their desired result (either making their wife laugh or insulting her).

After you have gained an understanding of the significance of dirty conversation, we will now discuss the two types...

The first category includes filthy and dirty conversation, which does not alter the way you experience sexuality. This ought to be avoided at all costs. A man who does not comprehend the significance of CONTEXT in the manner in which he communicates with his wife when they are at home is unable of avoiding making inappropriate comments. I am referring to the ability to know what to say, when to say it, how to say it, and when to communicate the significance of what you say.

The second category of dirty talk is meant to reinforce the many sexual encounters that take place in the bedroom between a man and his partner. You are going to become the kind of man who can make any lady happier than she could possibly have imagined possible, Master. You guys are the kind of men who can really go inside a woman's head and mess with her!

Please Describe Your Objectives And The Driving Forces Behind Them.

Make a covenant with one another to accept one another and take risks, regardless of what other people might think or say. Give one another total freedom to explore new interests without making the other feel obligated in any way, so that your partnership can thrive.

When you first meet someone, it's a great idea to talk about your preferences in terms of dirty talk, including what turns you on and what turns you off. If you ask the other person what their boundaries are before you meet, you will have a better idea of what is and is not acceptable. This will help put your mind at ease.

Your anxiety of dirty talking sex capers in the future will be significantly reduced as a result of this plain chat.

However, even having this discussion and being aware that it is okay to leap, your mind will continue to strive to keep you from moving ahead into the unknown.

If you find yourself in such a predicament, remember to breathe. Pay attention to the eyes of your spouse. Always keep in mind that they gave you their blessing. Remember how much they care about you and how much you can count on them to be there for you.

Break through the barrier in your throat to send a resounding "fuck you" to the illogical portion of your brain that tries to keep you back and prevents you from being entirely expressed, thoroughly seen, and genuinely loved.

Your level of trust and intimacy with your partner will rise to entirely new heights. If you can muster the fortitude to battle through these challenging times, not only will you emerge on the other side with increased self-assurance, but your relationship as a whole will also benefit in ways that you could not have anticipated.

Are you experiencing a great deal of fear? Send a text message to start your shady conversation.

If you are particularly nervous about beginning your foray into verbalized filthy talk, sending your spouse some unpleasant text messages and seeing their reaction is an ideal way to guage the scenario (and acquire more at ease with it).

If you have evidence in your mind that they appreciate it and want you to do it, you will feel a lot safer and more at ease conveying your dirty ideas in person. You may even find that you enjoy doing so.

In addition, sending each other sexually suggestive messages is an excellent way to ramp up the chemistry on dates or, if it already exists, to keep it alive.

Say whatever is on your mind, whether it be something that comes from the heart (or the crotch). This will give you some ideas of where to start.

How to Have Sexual Experiences Over the Phone in a Sassy and Tempting Way

Do you aspire to work as a sultry seductress over the phone? Do you want to make your girl's blood boil with your words and make her wish you were there with her at the moment she's experiencing it? Do you want to make a good impression on everyone you talk to, even if it takes a few minutes of dirty banter?

Continue reading, and in no time at all, you'll be an expert in the art of sex chat and phone sex, even if you've never had phone sex before. It doesn't matter if you've never had phone sex before.

If you simply follow these tips for phone sex, you will know everything there is to know in order to have a wild, sexual conversation with each other and completely arouse one another!

The importance of patience and mastering the art of phone sex

It is not possible to have phone sex in a hurry. Just like you require foreplay to experience powerful sex in bed, you need to practice patience and construct the scenario before you start talking negatively toward the other person.

A piece of advice for novices is that picking up the phone late at night will invariably result in the conversation feeling more seductive and passionate.

To get started, just drop your voice to the point where you are virtually whispering and keep talking. If your sweetheart asks you why you're whispering, you can either provide an explanation or indicate that you don't want to be overheard.

As soon as you lower your voice to a whisper, it is highly possible that your partner will begin to copy your voice and begin whispering as well—even if they are unaware that they are doing so!

Always keep in mind the importance of having patience, and schedule at least one hour of uninterrupted phone time for you and your partner every day.

You are not need to express your desire to have phone sex to your partner or place any kind of pressure on them to initiate the activity. Speak as you normally would, but keep your tone calm and your volume low, and the rest will take care of itself.

Creating the ideal atmosphere for sexual encounters over the phone

The setting in which you engage in phone sex can have a significant influence on how you feel overall and the degree to which you enjoy it. If you want to have a raunchy conversation without anyone interrupting you, you can make your environment more appropriate by following the advice in this article.

Dim the lights as much as you can.

The less distractions there are in the room, the better you'll be able to focus on what it is that you're hearing without losing your train of thought. Even being able to view your own body can sometimes be a source of distraction.

Put an end to the call that's been going on for a while now.
If you have the opportunity and the time, disable call waiting before you call your lover. You may even call them at an ungodly hour of the night, when you typically wouldn't be expecting any phone calls at all.

If you are on the phone with your significant other and a close friend contacts you multiple times while you are on the phone with them, it will undoubtedly disrupt the environment.

Make sure to leave a little space in between your eyelids.

If you close and lock the door behind you, you will isolate yourself from the other people and things in the world. You may either slouch back and unwind on the sofa, or you can get into bed and hide beneath the covers. Put absolutely all of your focus on the words that you are both saying and hearing right now.

There should be no music playing at all.

When you first start listening to music together, it may seem alluring and appropriate, but within a short while, it will become an annoying distraction because you won't be able to understand what your partner is saying.

Talk with a low voice.

If you want to initiate phone sex, never, ever, ever, ever, ever, ever, ever, ever, ever, ever, ever, ever, ever, ever, ever,

ever, ever, ever, ever, ever You should begin the call by speaking normally, but as the conversation continues, you should climb into bed, adopt a hoarse voice, and speak very quietly.

The more difficult it is for your discussion partner to hear what you are saying, the more involved they will become in what you are saying.

Your rate of speech needs to slow down.

You should not, under any circumstances, attempt to quicken the tempo of the discussion. When your spouse is feeling more comfortable and stimulated, you will naturally speak more slowly and become more relaxed as a result.

Put your own spin on it.

While you are conversing about anything else, make sure to call your significant other by their name or their pet name every once in a while. The entire contact is made more personal and sensual as a result of this.

Allow her to determine your worth on her own.

Let her uncover your awesomeness in the manner and at the pace that works best for her rather than rushing to brag about it all the time. The vast majority of guys hardly never consider whether or not the timing or placement is right. Who has more of an impact on you: a woman who tells you within the first ten minutes of meeting her that she is a model and has a lot of money, or a lady about whom you learn information much later and without her telling you?

Because the one asking the question does not know how much additional value is beyond the surface, the effect of the question becomes more significant as it requires the respondent to dig deeper for information.

A person who is a musician, an entrepreneur, or who has a doctorate is incredibly remarkable. But if they reveal that information right away, you might conclude that it is the thing that is most interesting about them. After that, you do not make any attempt to learn anything else about them since you assume that you have already heard the most important information about them.

If you needed to conduct research in order to learn that, it makes you wonder what other fascinating things you could possibly unearth in the process.

Many women entertain the fantasy that they are capable of "figuring out" a man on their own. They prefer to think that their own feminine intuition is some sort of superpower that can see through the stony and emotionless facades that others put up. They experience a rush of excitement whenever they come to the realization that they have picked up something valuable about you as a result of using that method.

In addition, she imagines herself falling in love with you long before she actually does so in reality. This indicates that you want her to be curious about you and to keep her mind focused on you at all times.

A Few Words About Giving Compliments

A man who compliments a woman on her appearance and does so in an overly flattering manner is doing one of the most damaging things he can possibly do to the relationship. If you have already read the book "Don't Be Simp-pathetic," then you are aware that you should not behave in such a manner. How exactly do you go about letting her know that you're interested in her in a way that isn't clingy or wimpy?

The point of this strategy is to offer a genuine complement while also making it very clear that you are not acting in the goal of receiving something in return. You do not want to give the impression that you are trying to get into her trousers by flattering her.

The art of flirting is always more successful than that of flattering. But what if she's dense (as some 9s and 10s are) and she doesn't pick up on the fact that you're trying to flirt with her? Sometimes you will need to explain things to her in more detail.

Complimenting her on something that is under her control is the most effective strategy for dealing with her. Tell her that you admire a particular decision that she has taken in regard to her beauty rather than simply complimenting her overall attractiveness, given that she was very much born that way. This could refer to the way she coordinated her wardrobe that day or the way she styled her hair on that particular day.

But instead of admiring her appearance, it is significantly more effective to commend her on things that pertain to her thinking, such as appreciating an idea that she comes up with, confirming a point of view that she has, or praising the good work that she has done or made. When a person has put more effort into anything, they will enjoy receiving compliments on that object more than they would otherwise.

Find something in her that you can sincerely admire, and then take the time to tell her why you appreciate it. Or, if the two of you share the same viewpoint on a certain subject, you may explain to her why you believe that viewpoint to be the correct one, as this is an effective method for establishing a connection.

One thing that a lot of males do that never ends well is to compliment someone on something you have reason to believe may make them feel horrible about themselves. It's usually those curvy, busty babes that are self-conscious about their weight, and he says something along the lines of preferring curvy chicks when they express their concerns about their appearance. Because their insecurity was obvious enough for you to notice it, this simply serves to make it worse for them when you do something like this.

Context is really important, and one aspect of that is who is making the statement. A person's reaction to a compliment from one man can be very different from how they react to the same compliment from another man.

Her opinion of him will have a role in how she evaluates what he has to say. What you have to say about her is always welcomed, whether or not she is already interested in you. However, if she finds you creepy, it will create an awkward and uncomfortable atmosphere.

If you want to avoid making her feel awkward in any way, it is better not to have any emotional investment in whether or not she responds well to what you have to say. In this way, it will not appear as if you are conducting a transaction in which you are trying to obtain something in return, such as attention.

Do not interrupt the conversation in order to wait for her to recognize what you have said. Instead, continue talking. This is the source of the uneasy tension in the situation. Instead, proceed directly to the next topic in your discussion. Many men utter words of adoration and adulation in the vain hope that the woman will like them, date them, or engage in sexual activity with them in return. When you put everything into perspective, that trade has to be the most unfair one in the history of human history. This is the primary reason why women do not date weaklings.

Continue the conversation instead by asking questions on whatever it is that you are emphasizing. What is the backstory behind her outfit, any noticeable scars, her clothes, her jewelry, her rings, her necklaces, and her tattoos?

Discuss sexuality and the state of your sexual health openly.

People typically have conversations about sexuality with their parents, friends, and romantic partners during the course of their life. The ability of young people to freely discuss topics such as birth control, condom use, and behaviors for which they are not adequately prepared preserves their health throughout their lifetimes. Put off your sexual debut till you feel ready. Abstinence is promoted as the only method that is 100 percent successful within comprehensive sexual health education. prevent HIV, STDs, and unintended pregnancies, and to acknowledge that this is a choice that everyone has the right to make. Dozens of sex education programs have been shown to be successful in assisting young people in delaying their first sexual experience or having fewer frequent sexual encounters. Gain an understanding of the differences between healthy and harmful relationships. Positive communication, conflict management, and the ability to negotiate decisions about sexual activity are all abilities that a significant number of young people never acquire, which makes maintaining a healthy relationship challenging. Inadequate development in these areas can put young people in relationships that are not only unhealthy but also potentially violent. Within the past twelve months, one out of every ten high school students has been the victim of physical abuse committed by a partner. Understanding and being able to distinguish between healthy and unhealthy relationship patterns should be a part of the curriculum for classes on sexual education. Strategies to avoid or leave an unhealthy relationship, as well as effective ways to communicate needs and manage conflict within the context of a relationship.

In addition to this benefit, sex education enables young people to investigate the factors that can either contribute to a positive or negative opinion of their bodies.

Honor the right of other people to maintain their own physical autonomy. Eight percent of high school students have reported being forced to have sexual relations, while one in ten students have admitted to engaging in sexually violent behavior. Young people should be taught what sexual violence is, why it is wrong, and how to receive help if they have been sexually attacked as part of a comprehensive and effective sexual education program.

Acquire an awareness of, an appreciation for, and a sense of ownership over your body. Comprehensive sexual health education not only teaches the foundations of adolescence and development, but it also enables young people to make choices about their behaviors and to say no to unwanted sexual activity. This is because the education not only teaches the fundamentals of adolescence and development, but it also teaches the fundamentals of sexual health.

Everyone deserves to be treated with dignity and respect, regardless of their sexual orientation or how they identify as a gender. People who identify as lesbian, gay, bisexual, or transgender (often referred to as LGBT) have made significant progress toward equality in recent decades. However, LGBT young people are still subject to harassment and prejudice. Eighty-two percent of LGBT students have been the target of bullying due to their sexual orientation, and 38 percent of LGBT students have been the target of physical bullying.

Ensure that your academic success is preserved. It is possible for a student's sexual health to influence their academic performance. Absenteeism and early school departure can be caused by a variety of factors, including health problems and unintended pregnancies.

How To Be A Master In The Art Of Flirting With Her

Texting a woman to show interest in them is something that a lot of men find difficult to accomplish. Because there are so many cues of interest that aren't present in a text exchange, it can be difficult for some guys to determine whether or not the woman they're texting is into them.

Your personality and the nature of the woman you are attempting to woo should both play a role in determining the manner in which you flirt with her. While some women enjoy being made fun of, others squirm at the very thought of it.

It is essential that you are able to feel confident in your masculinity in the presence of her and in your own flesh. If you are not at ease with yourself as a result of who you are or how she makes you feel, then this will come across in the message, and it will put her off. You should have confidence in who you are and not be scared to share your thoughts and feelings with a woman.

1. Use an effective first sentence.

It is important that the first message you send to her is a positive one since it will determine how the remainder of your interactions with her will proceed. The most effective method to begin a conversation is to ask a question that demonstrates that you have been paying attention and that you are interested in learning more about the person you are talking to.

Questions such as "What do you usually do in your free time, thinking about me?" Tell her that you are interested in what she is doing and that you hope she will continue to chat. If a woman sees that you are interested in who she is as a person and not simply in her physical appearance, she will appreciate you more.

If she needs a few minutes to think about it before answering, then give her that time to do so before continuing the conversation. The message should be succinct and straightforward, and you should strive to maintain a positive tone throughout. Do not discuss your previous sexual exploits, your occupation, or the activities you participated in that day with her.

Maintain your focus on the here and now and inquire about her day.

2. Get to Know Each Other

After you have succeeded in making her more open, the following stage is to engage in more personal conversation with her. To reiterate, it is not about you or what you did or did not do that day; rather, it is about what she did and what she wants out of life.

You can make it extremely personal by inquiring about her family and the ambitions she has for the future. You could inquire of her, "How is your father doing? Do you long for him at all? If she begins to tell you about her family and the place she spent her childhood, you should immediately inquire about the school she attended. In this way, in the event that the conversation becomes a little bit dull for any reason, the two of you will still have something to talk about.

3. Give her a little bit of a hard time.

If she starts to open up to you, you can then tease her a little bit to make her blush if you want to see her reaction. To tease someone is to flirt with them in a way that is light-hearted and amusing.

If she like the things you are making fun of her about, she will likely make fun of you as well. If she teases you back, then you can be sure that she is interested in being with you and that she is turned on by you. Maintain a playful and light-hearted tone with her, and make it clear that you are not in the least bit serious about what you are saying.

You never fail to make me feel like I have butterflies in my stomach whenever I think about you.

4. Don't be monotonous or predictable in your behavior.

Being overly casual and predictable will not get you anywhere, and it is the surest way to make a female lose interest in you as quickly as possible. Maintain a flirtatious and lighthearted tone throughout the message, but avoid anything sexual. You want her to be aware of your interest in her, but at the same time allowing her to determine how she feels about you. If a message appears to have been sent from a robot, then it is likely to be dull, and she is not going to want to chat to you about it.

5. Try not to take life so seriously.

You should not make the effort to be solemn all the time since it is impossible. She wants the same thing that you do, which is for you to open up to her and share more personal things with her.

If the tone of your message comes off as being very passionate or excessively serious, she is likely to get the impression that you are a creep. Do not send a message to a woman in which you discuss how difficult it was for you to get through your workday or how little sleep you had the night before. Women are typically turned off by guys who are needy and overly serious about everything in their lives. Therefore, you should not send a message in which you discuss these topics. Include a few of jokes or something else humorous into the conversation so that she can see that you are a fun-loving someone who enjoys having a good time.

6. Make a good impression on her by being optimistic.

It is imperative that you demonstrate that you are an upbeat and jovial individual. You can accomplish this goal by relating to her the events of your day, including how much fun you had, or by relating to her something positive that has occurred in your life. Women are drawn to males who can carry on conversations that are lighthearted, uplifting, and amusing.

If you send her messages that are constantly negative, she will believe that you are a downer, and if you send her messages that are always sad or gloomy, she will think that you have difficulties and troubles of your own. If your messages are always negative, she will think that you are a downer.

Don't talk about work and money like everyone else, which is boring and ordinary discourse that no one wants to hear. Maintain a pleasant attitude towards your day, and it will come across in the way that you talk to her.

7. Rely on pet names.

The employment of nicknames for her is an effective strategy for creating the impression that she is unique. The use of nicknames is a playful approach to flirt with a lady, and it also gives the impression that you are interested in her without appearing to be very upfront about it.

If you send a message to a person and address them by their nickname, it conveys two messages at once: first, that you are interested in getting to know the person, and second, that you are flirtatious. One example of the use of nicknames is as follows: Hello, beautiful. How did you spend your day?

8. Give her some room to catch up to you and pursue you.

Playing hard to get without being overly difficult is the most effective approach to have a woman chase after you. Maintain your composure and give her the opportunity to gain your love. If you give off the impression of being overly eager or needy, then you will drive her away even more quickly than she did with the previous person who wrote her a message.

You need to have self-assurance if you want her to be drawn to you, and she will be more attracted to you if she feels you are the prize. If she has to work extra hard to catch your attention, it's because you're not easy to get. Always remember that women appreciate the thrill of the chase, and if she thinks that she has to put in extra effort to get your attention, then that will only make her want it even more. When you've succeeded in capturing her attention, you can move in closer to her in preparation for a time when the two of you can enjoy yourself while engaging in sexual activity.

9. Don't let your religion consume you.

It is essential for a guy to be truthful and true in all interactions, yet there are some things that he can keep to himself. A woman won't want to talk to a man who is fixated on religion or politics since she won't find him interesting. Because women have their own thoughts and convictions on the matter at hand, it is recommended that you refrain from expressing yours unless she specifically asks you what it is that you believe in.

How do you explain to your partner that you are interested in trying something different?

You will get the desired outcome if you talk to your lover about the sexual fantasy you had a few days ago, but if you need additional pressure, you can always try other things. Consider the question, "Is this something that we can investigate together?"

How to pick up were we left off in the chat later

Now that you have shared your plans with your significant other, everything appears to be running smoothly. However, what steps should you take next? The importance of honesty cannot be overstated in any facet of a romantic partnership. The most effective method of conveying whether or not a desire is sexual is to be forthright and forthrightly honest.

I ask that you maintain this practice going forward. Would you be interested in trying something new, even though it's something you've been saying you don't like? Or, would you say that you truly enjoy it? It is essential that we have an open channel of communication at all times because we have earned the right to feel like partners when we are having sexual relations.

What should I do if it seems like my spouse has lost interest in having sexual relations with me?

According to research, sexual gratification plays a crucial part in maintaining successful relationships. However, there are a number of elements that influence the quality of a couple's sexual life as well as an individual's sexual desire during the course of a relationship. It's possible to have any kind of connection. Your spouse may experience dryness if they suddenly go through a period in which they have a lower interest in sex than you do.

It's possible that your partner is experiencing temporary difficulties as a result of the stress at work or other things that are hurting them.

It is not uncommon for the spouse to become weary as a result of the unexpected and hectic schedule (which may include end-of-year examinations or deadlines) and be unable to do anything other than take a sleep or spend the night in front of the television.

These dry spells occur frequently and vanish on their own once the situation has reached a stable state. Long-term or hazy sexual desires can be detrimental to a relationship as well as to the overall health and happiness of both partners. Not only may this lead to feelings of frustration and self-doubt, but it may also cause you to question if this is the first step toward a marriage that lacks sexual intimacy.

This worry is not completely without basis in reality. According to recent research, the number of persons who engage in sexual activity is on the decline. No matter their gender, color, or marital status, American adults are having fewer sexual encounters, according to the findings of a study that was just published in the Archives of Sexual Behavior.

Challenges faced

There is no hard and fast rule that dictates what constitutes a "too long" dry order. It is important to consider the age of both partners, the length of time they have spent together, as well as their general sexual practices. It is essential to avoid getting the "medium" notes and the level of normalcy of the relationship confused with one another. Every single person is unique in their own way. But the most essential issue is whether or not you are content with the amount and quality of sex you are getting.

Last but not least, action needs to be made when a dry spell places a visible strain on the relationship or affects the confidence of either one or both of the partners. And doing so can be challenging. If neither partner is willing to be truthful and open with the other, any conversation regarding the couple's inability to have sexual relations is likely to result in feelings of guilt, wrath, or shame rather than in the discovery of a solution.

To that end, there are several steps that you and the other people involved can do to remedy the problem. You begin by arguing that it is not possible to anticipate whether or not your spouse has sexual preferences that can be assumed.

Reason for

It is normal practice to minimize the importance of gender and intimacy. According to a number of studies, the reduction in sexual intimacy begins around the age of 45 and continues as people get older. 3. three

A lack of desire in sexual activity can be caused by a number of different things. Therefore, if you have any reason to believe that your partner is cheating on you, is gay, or is simply losing interest in the relationship, you should remain open to all of the options.

In addition to this, it is essential to differentiate between low libido (loss of libido), hypo-libido (lack of sexual fantasy), and sexual dysfunction. Both the physical and psychological factors may be to blame, but the treatments for each condition are very distinct. If you have a clear understanding of the distinctions, you will be better able to look at problems in an objective manner and steer clear of many emotional implications.

a lack of libido

A decrease in interest in sexual activities is one of the symptoms of low libido. If the underlying cause can be identified, then treatment may be an option.

A decline in sexual interest may have many origins, including the following:

Tension and Mood Disorders

Dysfunction of the erection

Incorrect levels of hormones (as a result of menopause and hypogonadism).

Pain felt in the genital region, such as that caused by vaginitis or balanitis.

persistent illness

Treatments and Medications

Low regard for oneself

Issues with interpersonal connections

The list might go on forever. Your desire for sex might be negatively impacted by a variety of mental issues as well.

a condition characterized by low libido

A person who suffers from hypoactive sexual dysfunction disorder (HSDD) does not have sexual fantasies or the urge to engage in sexual activities. It affects 8.9% of women between the ages of 18 and 44, 12.3% of women between the ages of 45 and 64, and 7.4% of women aged 65 and older and is the most frequent form of sexual dysfunction in women.

Research has shown that having HSDD is connected with a number of unfavorable consequences, such as a lower quality of life in terms of one's health, an increase in the frequency of negative emotions, lower levels of happiness, and lower levels of contentment with one's spouse. The illness is still neither identified nor treated, despite the fact that it has negative effects on people's lives. Fewer than half of people who have sexual issues visit a medical professional for assistance. Additionally, many people start talking about sexual issues because they are embarrassed or uncomfortable.

Sexual impotence or dysfunction

Sexual dysfunction refers to any condition that manifests itself at any moment in the sexual response cycle and impedes the ability of a person or a couple to have a sexual encounter that is fulfilling to them. Problems with desire, arousal, orgasm, or even pain could fall under this category.

Erectile dysfunction, delayed ejaculation, and premature ejaculation are all examples of different types of sexual dysfunction that can affect males. This type of sexual dysfunction can affect women, and it manifests itself as either a lack of lubrication during sexual activity or an inability to relax the vaginal muscles sufficiently to allow for sexual activity.

an Open and Transparent Method for Challenging the Wall

If you want to be the most approachable and influential source of sexual counseling for your child, you should be authentic while you are educating them about sex and sexuality. This will enhance the possibilities that you will. In our own unique ways, everyone of us might be considered a sexual educator.

The fact that we are parents compels us to do so, and we have an obligation to be forthright in the guidance that we provide to our offspring, just as I do with the educators that I prepare to instruct students in sexuality education. This indicates that in order to properly educate our children, we need to take them to an authentic setting.

Method of crossing the street that involves looking in both directions before doing so

Think about the methods you used to teach your child (or will use) how to cross the street safely. That is to say, you should expect to have a number of conversations about crossing the street at the corner, checking in both directions before entering the street, and crossing when the light is green.

You are going to act out a number of different scenarios that she might go through while crossing the street, imitating different events that might really take place.

For instance, a driver may run a red light; she may arrive at a large crossroads where multiple vehicles want to turn at the same time; she may come at an intersection where the only lights are stop signs; you will construct every potential situation that your child may experience when crossing the street. You will, of course, take her outside onto the street so that she may become used to crossing it in the correct and safe manner.

When you do this, you will be providing your kid with authentic instruction (for more information, see the sidebar), which means that you will be teaching her by having her practice the skills that you want her to master.

What exactly does it mean to have Authentic Teaching?

A type of education that strives to be as accurate a representation of actual life experiences as possible, authentic instruction is sometimes referred to as authentic teaching. Learning by doing is an essential component of authentic education even in its most fundamental form. If you want to teach someone how to climb a rock wall, you should have them get some practice doing it first.

If you are teaching your child how to cross the street, you can practice doing so with him by walking across the street with him. It is true that it is more difficult to teach your child about sexuality by using real-life situations (you can't really have sex with your child, can you?). However, this does not mean that it is impossible. However, there are a variety of different approaches that can be taken in order to recreate circumstances that occur in the real world.

For each of the topics that we are going to cover throughout the course of this book, such as sexual feelings, the influence of peers on sexual decision-making, and the differences between being a man and a female, I will give you with real-life examples of effective training techniques.

Think About a Situation That Actually Occurred

When it comes to educating your child about sex and sexuality, you should go as close as possible to having him experience what you want him to understand. This will help your child retain the information better. So, if you want your ten-year-old to understand how to avoid being sexually pressured by his peers, you should imagine that he is in middle school and that drop-dead gorgeous girl is coming on to him at a friend's home party: "What are you going to do when she tells you you're hot, touches your buttocks, and wants you to come with her and her friends to another party at someone else's house?" you inquire with him. "Your heart is pounding, you have butterflies in your stomach, and your pulse is rushing because you're so thrilled she's noticed you and no one else." Even more impressive, you now have an erection. "So, what are your plans?"

Since he is only ten years old, it is likely that he will act as though he is clueless. You will therefore take him through a number of different options for resolving this issue before coming to the conclusion that you hope he will come to, which is to refrain from engaging in any sexual activity.

You are going to reassure him that all of his feelings are normal, but that ultimately he needs to make a choice that reduces the likelihood of a sexual encounter happening between the two of you.

This scenario is a good explanation of how you may approach the concept of "ten is the new sixteen" with your child who is ten years old. Consider using it as a guide while communicating with your child. Because children of this age are not typically subjected to the influence of their peers, it might be challenging for a youngster as young as ten to fully appreciate a circumstance such as this one.

However, rather than waiting until your child is thirteen or fourteen years old to begin teaching them about these things, you should start doing so right away when they are 10 years old. It is important to keep in mind that it is far simpler to instill the idea of sexual abstinence in youngsters who have very little or no interest in actually having sex with one another than it is to try to do so later in life when interest begins to grow.

Let's take a look at another illustration of authentic training, shall we? Your daughter, who is six years old, has expressed concern to you about a male in her class who has repeatedly attempted to touch her buttocks and the space between her legs.

He has also experimented with it with some of the other children who are enrolled in her class. Notify her that notifying you was the appropriate thing to do, and that she should always tell the instructor if he tries to touch her. Also, let her know that she should tell you if the teacher tries to touch her.

Tell her that you will discuss it with the instructor as well as the principal, and that all three of them will collaborate to ensure that he does not engage in the behavior again. You explain to her that some children have trouble keeping their hands to themselves, and that they do it to draw attention or to make themselves feel bigger and better than the other children. You also tell her that some children have trouble keeping their hands to themselves because they do it to feel superior to the other children. "The next time he attempts to do this to you, tell him 'no' in a forceful voice and go notify your teacher," advises the instructor. You can tell him that you'll work with him or play a game with him if he wants to, but that you won't let him touch you. " You and your daughter can act out many scenarios in which the boy is appropriate in his interactions with her and when he tries to touch her. For example, you can tell him that you'll work with him or play a game with him if he wants to. Pretend that you are your daughter and act out how she would respond to each situation. Educating students about sexuality and sex through the use of role-playing is a tried-and-true strategy.

When it comes to their academic and social pursuits, girls consistently demonstrate high levels of precision, diligence, and perseverance.

Girls are more likely to sketch homes, trees, and flowers, whereas guys are more likely to depict garages, automobiles, and airplanes. Girls are more likely to focus on a person's clothing, accessories, and haircut when drawing them, as opposed to boys, who tend to show people in more broad terms or as soldiers with all of their gear.

Those educators who do the right thing by seating boys and girls at the same desk are those teachers. The result is that girls talk less and boys make less noise. Girls tend to be more conscientious in their academic pursuits, which helps drag guys along with them. A significant number of guys develop into quieter, more focused individuals. It is common knowledge that boys have a higher IQ, are more self-reliant, and do not give up easily, while girls are known to be more accurate, diligent, responsive, sensitive, and compassionate. Therefore, the proximity of boys and girls sitting at a desk together helps create and develop morally beneficial comradely bonds between them, and it also occasionally avoids excessively displayed sexual one-sidedness. Girls are growing less self-conscious and more authentic, whereas boys are getting more kind, gentler, more polished.

With the commencement of schooling, suitable conditions are established for the education of boys of true male nobility, which is essential for imagining the future youth and man. Without it, it is difficult to picture the future. The raising of male nobility should be continually and firmly pursued by parents, utilizing their example and the examples of those around them. Parents should use their own examples and the examples of others around them. It is essential to instill in the kid a cautious and sensitive attitude towards his grandmother, mother, sister, and in general, all girls. This should start with the child's own mother and then go on to his grandmother and mother. It is necessary to make it clear to the young man that his mother, who he adores very much, is actually yesterday's girl. And the woman who sits next to him at the desk will be the mother of his child. Therefore, the wonderful emotion that unites the kid with his mother becomes the norm for forming relationships with girls as a standard.

The bow may be pulled and pushed by the youngster as he is having fun. There is nothing to worry about in this location. It is a far more serious matter if the boy does not carry out his responsibility and does not safeguard the young lady. A younger kid should be aware that it is improper and exceedingly low on the totem pole to insult a female.

While they were both playing in the yard, Vova struck the girl.

The man's shocked question to his son was, "Did you hit the girl?" "So, you are able to put up a fight against your mother?"

Son trying to hide his embarrassment bowed his head.

— She was the first one to climb! He mumbled something.

— I have no interest in hearing justifications from a future guy who defends himself in such an embarrassing manner! — The father exploded in rage and stormed up to the front door. And the son, hiding his eyes under his brows, glanced after him as he walked away, and then, carefully selecting his words, he apologized to the girl. The females never again voiced their concerns regarding him.

It is essential for children of both sexes to have supportive social networks if they are to develop healthy, satisfying interactions with one another. Parents have the responsibility of ensuring that their children maintain healthy friendships with both males and females of the same and other sexes, as well as preventing their children from treating their relationships with these friends in a careless and self-centered manner. It is important for parents to be aware of the people their children spend time with and the activities in which they participate. They should also make sure that their children's time is filled with stimulating activities such as intriguing talks, games, and book discussions.

Making Use of Sexual Interactions in Order to Manipulate Emotions

To reiterate, sexual communication is the universal language of understanding between women. You might be surprised to learn that sexual communication is not always about sex; nonetheless, it typically leads to sex at some point in the relationship. There are no hard and fast regulations, the only requirement being that you come out on top. In order to improve your skills in sexual communication, consider the following guidelines:

Figure Out How to Whisper.

Sometimes it is the most gentle of voices that may bring even the most resolute of hearts to their knees. In addition to this, whispering gets more attention than speaking normally would; otherwise, she won't be able to understand what you are saying. Here is a helpful hint: Use the fact that you are in a noisy place as an excuse to whisper in her ear, and as you are doing so, let your lips to brush against her ear in a nonchalant way.

Refrain From Going All In

ones, particularly attractive ones, are accustomed to having a large number of admirers from an early age. Don't lay all of your cards on the table just yet; instead, make her wonder why, out of everyone in the room, you are the only one who views her as a person and not a goddess. This causes her to feel insecure and compels her, in some way, to demonstrate her worth to you.

Take Some Chances

Women appreciate men who aren't afraid to try new things. A good woman does not figuratively fall in love with a bad person; rather, she falls in love with the behaviors that a bad guy engages in, such as being unreasonable and taking risks. Why? because women need novelty in their lives and want to try new things. People with really vibrant spirits take risks even when they know they could fail, and she finds this to be a highly fascinating trait in others.

Do Not Provide Exact Details. What's Going Through Your Head

Women enjoy being taken by surprise. Because of this, you should never give her permission to read your mind, at least not totally. Keep in mind what Albert Einstein had to say about beauty: "The most beautiful thing we can encounter is the mystery. It is the origin of all genuine artistic endeavors and scientific research.

www.ingramcontent.com/pod-product-compliance
Lightning Source LLC
Chambersburg PA
CBHW050239120526
44590CB00016B/2156